Making A Movie

Contents   **Page**

written by John Lockyer

These people are in a cinema. They are sitting in rows, looking at a large, dark screen. Some of them are having drinks, while others are eating popcorn. Everyone is waiting, feeling excited.

Suddenly the lights go out and the room gets quiet. The people see pictures moving on the screen. They hear music and voices. The movie has started!

Movies use moving pictures and sound to tell stories. Some stories have been made up, while others are about real people and real places and things. The stories can be funny, scary, interesting or exciting.

4

Most movies are made so that they can be shown on a big screen. Let's find out how a movie is made.

The story of a movie is called a script. When a script is finished, a producer gets all the money that is needed to make the movie. He also finds people to work on the movie.

The actors read the script to find out about the story. They must remember all the words that they have to say in the movie. They must learn how to move, and what kind of voice to use, too.

The director reads the script many times, so that he can show the actors how to play their parts. When everyone knows what to do, the director shouts, "Action!"

While the actors move about and say their words,
a cameraman takes moving pictures of them.
Sometimes many cameramen work on the same movie.

An editor puts all the moving pictures together. Then the director and the editor work out which parts of the movie are the most interesting and exciting. They cut out anything they don't want.

Music and singing are recorded by sound operators, who join it with the moving pictures. After the titles are added, the movie is finished and ready to show.

Some movies have special effects. When a superhero flies, that is a special effect. Explosions are made to look real. Dangerous stunts, like crashing cars, are also special effects.

Movies about space use computers to make their special effects. The computers draw pictures of space, alien worlds, alien creatures, and spaceships. The pictures are so good that they look real.

Computers are also used to make animated movies. For these movies, many pictures are taken of special drawings. The drawings in each picture look a little bit different.

The computer puts the pictures together one after another, and then plays them at a fast speed. The things in the drawings look as if they are moving. A cartoon is an animated movie.

People in every part of the world watch movies. Not all of them go to the cinema. People watch movies at home, outdoors, in planes, in cars, and even in space!